CHRIS BONINGTON'S

Lake District

The Coniston Fells are reflected in the
early morning stillness of Kelly Head
Tarn on Torver Back Common. Photo by
Val Corbett.

CHRIS BONINGTON'S
Lake District

In association with the National Trust

First published in Great Britain 1997 by
Dalesman Publishing Company Limited
Stable Courtyard
Broughton Hall
Skipton
North Yorkshire BD23 3AE

Text and photographs © Chris Bonington, Val Corbett, Julie Fryer,
David W Jones, Brian Hibbert

A British Library Cataloguing in Publication record is available for
this book

ISBN 1 85568 120 X

Designed by Jonathan Newdick
Typeset by SPAN Graphics Limited
Colour Origination by RCS Digital Graphics
Printed by Midas Printing (HK) Limited

Contents

Ennerdale is one of the wildest and most attractive valleys in the Lake District. Its natural glacial lake has supplied water for over 140 years and today supplies the communities of Whitehaven and Copeland. A new treatment works was needed to maintain safe supplies and meet ever-increasing customer demand. The works has been built mostly underground, using tunnelling techniques to protect the beauty of the valley. The control centre, built in local stone, is disguised as a farm building.

Foreword by North West Water

North West Water has a key role as a custodian in the Lake District, working in partnership to protect this area of natural beauty for the benefit of those who live, work and visit, as well as for future generations.

We provide water and wastewater services to seven million people in the north west of England. Our role in the Lake District is to collect, clean and distribute vital water. Around one third of the region's daily water comes from the catchment areas around Haweswater, Thirlmere and Ennerdale. Here reservoirs and surrounding areas are managed and protected, to deliver quality drinking water and preserve the natural beauty and wildlife habitats.

A crucial aspect of our role is to balance the increasing demand for water with the desire for conservation, access and recreation. We will continue to improve access for people to enjoy walking, fishing and observing wildlife, whilst preserving the quality of the water and recognising the needs of the environment.

We work in partnership with the British Trust for Conservation Volunteers, Cumbria Wildlife Trust, English Nature, Lake District National Park Authority, National Trust, Royal Society for the Protection of Birds and our farming tenants. We have a long-term commitment to community partnerships and recently celebrated twenty-one years of working with BTCV – conserving and rebuilding footpaths, dry stone walls and planting trees.

As part of our commitment to enhancing children's learning and understanding of the Lake District, we have opened, in partnership with the Lake District National Park, the Brockhole Environmental Education Centre. This is part of our network of education centres in the north west, visited by more than 7,000 children a year to learn about the value of water in our lives.

It is because of our role in the Lake District that we are delighted to support this book which recognises and celebrates the beauty of this special place.

My Lake District by Chris Bonington

The Lake District has played a major part in my life from almost as far back as I can remember. My introduction to its hills began at the age of five, when the school I was attending in London was evacuated to Kirkby Lonsdale on the southern fringes of the Lake District. During that time I spent the holidays in Grasmere and Elterwater with my grandmother and even though I didn't discover climbing until I was sixteen, she took me walking and my love of the fells was born. I can still remember scrambling up beside the tumbling Sour Milk Ghyll to Easedale Tarn, picnicking on White Moss Common and boating on Grasmere.

In fact, a lot of my early climbing was in Wales and Scotland, and between 1951, when I started climbing, and 1960, I visited the Lakes only once, preferring to rush north to the rugged crags of Scotland. However, I gradually came to appreciate the softer, gentle beauty of the Lakes and began to visit more frequently. I have memories of many wonderful days spent rock climbing, not only on the high dramatic crags of the Central Fells but on the red sandstone cliffs at St Bees, the granite of Eskdale and the classic crags of Borrowdale.

One such day was in the summer of 1962. I was climbing with an old friend, Ian MacNaught-Davis. It was a glorious day but for some reason we had a lazy morning and only after lunch tackled North Crag Eliminate, an extreme route on Castle Rock in St John's in the Vale. We completed this by three o'clock, but felt vaguely dissatisfied, even though it had been a fine route. We thought that as it was such a beautiful day we should have gone to a high crag, so decided there and then to do just that. We hurriedly drove to the top of Honister Pass and set off at four o'clock for Pillar Rock, traversing the head of Ennerdale below Gable and along the high level track to Pillar. We chose the North North West route, a delightful classic, very severe, and started up it at six pm. We still had time to complete the route, rush back to Honister, drive down Borrowdale and reach the Scafell Hotel for a pint of beer just before closing.

It was perhaps this day that gave me the idea of living in the Lakes. The thought that I could fit into a long summer afternoon and evening what would have been a full day in its own right, made me realise how much climbing I could get if I lived in the area. So, in 1962, soon after I had made the first British ascent of the North Wall of the Eiger and Wendy and I had been married, we were looking for somewhere to live. She had been brought up in Sussex but did not mind where we lived as long as it was in the country. Six months in a furnished room in Hampstead had been enough of London living for her.

I was attracted to the Lake District, partly because I perhaps knew Wales too well, having spent two years at the Army Outward Bound School at Tywyn, but I also loved the softer beauty of the Lakeland scenery. So we settled for that and set off from London with our Minivan loaded with all our possessions. We thought we would easily find a delightful country cottage, with roses round the door, to rent for next to nothing, quite forgetting that nearly all such properties are let for holidays at much more than we could afford to pay.

We stayed with friends in Keswick and chased around looking at everything that was available. We had just about given up hope when a chance encounter with a climber, who was working in the bar at the Royal Oak in Ambleside, put us on the track of another possibility. It was a single room over a garage on a farm. He warned us that it was pretty rough. We set off straight away and drove to Loughrigg Farm to see if the room was still vacant. The farmer also warned us that 'it was a bit rough' and it was. I described it in my book Next Horizon.

'An outdoor staircase led up from the farmyard to a small balcony. A peeling wooden door opened into a fair-sized room, lit by a couple of windows. The walls were of bare plaster, brown with dirt, and traced with a network of cracks. The floor was covered with rotting linoleum, which had long lost its colour, and the room was furnished with a few pieces of battered furniture that had probably been rescued from a refuse dump. The nearest water was from a tap in the yard and the sanitary facilities were limited to an earth closet, the most primitive and smelly

Wasdale boasts one of the most spectacular dale heads with fine mountains crowding round the end of the Lake. To the left Yewbarrow resembles an upturned Viking longship or the back of a sleeping dragon, while in the centre the pyramid of Great Gable, symbol of the national park, demands attention. The Scafells, England's highest mountains, are hidden to the left but they ease the shoulder of Lingmell into the valley, while Wastwater's famous Screes plunge directly into the lake.

Borrowdale is a climber's valley with plenty of low-level crags close to the road and handy for an evening's climbing or snatching a route from the end of a rainy day.

of all toilets, placed at the back of a pigsty. Set in the backstreets of a city it would have been unbelievably sordid but here, in the heart of some of the most beautiful country either of us had ever lived in, it didn't seem to matter . . .

'From the balcony outside the door we could gaze across the farmyard, over the spring green grass of a field, dotted with clusters of Scots pine and larch, to the still waters of Loughrigg Tarn. . . . We lived in Loughrigg for three months and were able to watch the explosion of colour of every shade of green that takes place each spring in this part of the Lake District.'

From our first days at Loughrigg we fell in love with the Lakes and apart from a six-year spell in the Manchester area, we have lived there ever since.

From Loughrigg we moved to the Lodge at Woodland Hall in the south-west corner of the Lakes between Broughton-in-Furness and Coniston. It was comparatively unknown to the majority of tourists, a backwater, set slightly apart from the bigger hills of the Lakes but with views of Coniston Old Man and the rocky ridge of Caw and the Dunnerdale Fells. It isn't grand, awe-inspiring scenery, but neither is it pastoral. There is an intimacy about its tree-clad valleys, winding their way into craggy fells. Wendy and I came to love the changing colours and tones of the bracken-clad hillsides. After two years there we moved on to an unfurnished cottage near the foot of Ennerdale and eventually bought a house in Cockermouth, before moving to Manchester for a short spell.

Most of my major expeditions have been planned in the Lake District and it's a place I never tire of coming home to after the rigours of an expedition. It doesn't matter where I have been climbing, from the Himalayas to Greenland, Antarctica or the Alps; there is always a tremendous thrill when I first glimpse the Lakeland hills as I drive north up the M6. To me they are as beautiful as anywhere in the world with their amazing variety of form, the combination of lakes, crags and woodland with the infinite tones of green and brown contrasting with the rocky outcrops.

Our home for the last 24 years has been on the edge of the Northern Fells and I have become particularly fond of them because they have an identity of their own which separates them from the central and southern Lakes. The hills are more gentle and rolling, and the views are exceptional. Looking out from High Pike you can see north across the flat Solway Plain to the hills of Galloway, south to the main Lakes, or east across the Eden Valley to the spine of the Pennines. I must have climbed High Pike a thousand times but never tire of the view.

Wendy and I have, over the years, explored the less crowded corners of the Lakes. Even on a Bank Holiday, you can find places where you hardly see a single person all day. I enjoy picking a route off the map, usually around the periphery of the Lakes, which I hope will give us the mountains to ourselves, will yield pleasant views and give a rounded, enjoyable walk. There is a special pleasure in visualising the nature of the walk from the map and then seeing how close it comes to expectation. Our dog, or dogs, have always been essential companions on these explorations. We have had four over the years – a Staffordshire bull terrier called Bessie and three lovely mongrels, Bodie, Bella and Jess.

One of the joys of living in the Lakes is going out climbing on the long summer evenings at the end of a day's writing or having been on the telephone organising my next expedition. A few phone calls and I can usually find a fellow climber, often one who is self-employed like myself. Forty-five minutes' drive and you can get to most places in the northern Lakes, a short walk from the road in Borrowdale or Thirlmere; choose a west facing crag and you can climb on warm rock in the evening sun. I have even driven round to Wasdale and walked up Brown Tongue to Scafell Crag, to race the orb of the sun dropping down into the Irish Sea on one of the long classics of the crag.

One of the things that especially attracts me is the influence of man on the landscape. People have lived in the Lake District since earliest times, and since those times their activities have shaped the landscape. Even the most remote areas have been affected by man, the fell grass grazed short by the hardy hill sheep and the dry stone walls, so typical of the Lakes, winding their way over the fells. Whitewashed farms and stone built barns nestle in the valleys. The influence of man has mostly been harmonious but over the last twenty years, since we first came to live here, the pressure imposed by the ever-increasing number of tourists and the proliferation of activities, such as mountain biking, paragliding and so on, is causing problems, particularly of footpath erosion and over-crowded roads and car parks.

I feel there is a space for quiet enjoyment by all but with the increased use must come increased responsibility. All users of the fells must respect certain guidelines and develop a greater awareness of the impact being made on the environment, keeping this to a minimum, and ideally leaving no trace of their presence. The benefits we get from the hills are more than just recreation. They offer the chance to recharge our batteries in lives that are increasingly stressed and influenced by technology. The solution must not, however, be to limit the numbers of

Below. Elterwater is one of the smallest lakes, often overlooked and easily missed by those rushing up Langdale. They miss some delightful woodland scenery in an often quiet setting.

Opposite. Striding Edge is the high road to Helvellyn in every sense. In summer it is a fine airy route to the summit but under winter snow and ice it becomes almost Alpine and demands special care and skill.

Grasmoor, above Crummock Water, is the giant of the Buttermere Valley. Other fells, such as Fleetwith Pike at the head of the valley, can draw the eye with their shape but Grasmoor commands attention by it sheer overbearing bulk which dominates the north eastern wall of the valley and offers would-be challengers only forbiddingly steep slopes.

people going into the hills. Quite apart from being difficult to implement, our need for the inspiration and refreshment they provide is growing rather than reducing. The challenge is to find ways of enabling people to pursue their activities without spoiling the very place they use.

Footpath erosion has become a major problem in the Lake District, especially to the highest and most popular peaks such as Scafell Pike, Helvellyn and Great Gable, as well as in Langdale, Borrowdale and Buttermere. I was delighted, therefore, to be asked to be President of the National Trust Lake District Appeal. It was a chance to help raise money for the repair and upkeep of footpaths in the area which has given me so much since my first visit back in 1940 and has been my home for more than twenty years. The National Trust manages a large proportion of the central and grandest part of the national park under heaviest pressure from outdoor enthusiasts. It has been carrying out a programme of building and repairing footpaths on routes affected by erosion, using the available local stone without the addition of mortar or artificial materials, to enable people to enjoy the fells without destroying them.

With this sensitive and firm management by the National Trust (and also the National Park Authority), it should be possible for the many pressures on the environment to be balanced, allowing the cherished free access to the fells to remain, not only for us but for future generations.

VAL CORBETT

Chasing Rainbows

Val Corbett came to the North West in the late sixties to take a degree in religious studies at Lancaster University. Choosing to stay in the area afterwards, she tried a variety of jobs before discovering a talent for photography that rapidly developed into full-time work. Her photographs are extensively published in this country and around the world. She now lives in Helton on the eastern fringe of the Lake District with her husband and two daughters. In retrospect she should perhaps have chosen to live on the western fringe, the better to observe the arrival of the next change in the weather.

Heavy rain mixed with sleet brought an early end to my day doing voluntary work for the National Park, but this time the fickle weather improved enough for me to photograph this scene of shifting conditions on my way home alongside Ullswater.

Rain, as synonymous with the Lake District as Wordsworth or Kendal Mint Cake. The sheer abundance of the rainfall animates the exquisite diversity of streams, rivers and waterfalls that in turn replenish the tarns and lakes.

For a while the Border TV weather forecast was sponsored by the waterproof fabric makers, Goretex, an association that speaks volumes. My own experience with the Lake District began at the age of ten during a family holiday, faithfully recorded in my five-year diary. Our Hereford-shire farm was in a terrible state, brown grass parched by the scorching summer of 1959, and we drove north for ten hours. No wonder I recorded: 'How thrilling was the Preston bypass.' A week of thorough soakings followed and I have a sad entry of being hopelessly lost in the mist on Cat Bells, stoically singing He Who Would Valiant Be until rescued by my father.

Decades later, the capriciousness of the weather has become a matter of professional interest. Exasperating at times, its sheer fickleness does add great strength to the potential for landscape photography. I am driven by the brilliant cold light and billowing clouds brought by a north-westerly, the clarity of light that follows the clearance of rain, and the temperature inversions that leave a lake dreamily mantled in mist.

I like to seek out those slight shifts from bland to subtle light that transform a landscape. I most cherish those moments when a lake is perfectly still and richly lit.

To protect my sanity I gave up chasing rainbows a long while back. Nevertheless it takes a peculiar form of doggedness to catch these magical times. There is also the exasperation of wasted journeys and hours of lost time. Waiting has its own frustrations, always knowing that in the next valley conditions could be exactly right. However, when everything comes together the sense of achievement is heavenly. Mean-while, the frequent near-misses happen in sublime surroundings, even in the rain!

The chilly interior of St Martin's, the old church of Martindale, is not a cosy place to shelter from a rainstorm but its quiet simplicity makes it a church I particularly like to visit. The old leaded windows, here bespattered with rain, give views up Martindale to The Nab, home to a deer herd. The roar of stags rutting in the autumn can be quite alarming!

Outside the church, the little walled graveyard is shaded on one side by an ancient yew – said by some to be over 1,300 years old – and is cheerful with daffodils in spring.

Roaming the slopes of Hallin Fell and looking at Martindale, and its neighbour Boredale, mapped out beneath me is one of my most pleasurable short outings.

Despite its mundane name, the bogbean carries frilly flower spikes which look improbably ornate, especially seen in its normal habitat in shallow peaty pools. In contrast, the quiet qualities of reeds and rushes are easily overlooked.

There is only one way of taking photographs of water lilies such as these in Brotherswater. It involves getting wet. Fortunately, a tripod comes in handy to help with balance when trying to get secure footing in amongst the oozing mud and serpentine roots of the lilies. I try hard not to think about eels.

Looking south against the light of Blea Tarn, with the Coniston Fells as a backdrop.

Waiting on Side Pike during a bitterly cold and blustery day for dramatic panoramic photographs of the Great Langdale valley, became a desperate business. The light over the valley floor and the Pikes never 'came right' and I had had enough of continually crawling under a stunted holly for protection against the succession of hailstorms. But while retreating to my car I saw what was, on this particular day, the better image.

Pages 26 and 27. The favourite way of celebrating my birthday on November 1st is a walk, followed by tea in one of those Lake District hotels with huge chintzy settees, a roaring log fire and a groaning feast of sandwiches, scones and cakes. The mandatory walk differs only from my normal 'work', in that Tony, my husband, carries the cameras. It was on one such day, walking around Little Langdale, that these photographs were taken from Lingmoor Fell and of Bridge End Farm with the Langdales behind.

CHRIS BONINGTON'S LAKE DISTRICT

Early rising is not one of my natural attributes, and I will only undertake it when settled high pressure more or less guarantees a calm and sunny morning. Watching the delicate effects of mist rising from a lake, such as here on Ullswater, does make it worthwhile.

The boat landings at Keswick on Derwentwater are lit on good summer evenings by gorgeously rich low sun. It is a good spot to dally among the groups of tourists at the water's edge, and feel part of the holiday atmosphere.

Rowing or taking the launch must be a better way of appreciating Derwentwater than driving round on the congested roads. Boat trips also reveal the intricate islets and bays that are particularly characteristic of the Keswick end of the lake.

Left. Scale Force has the highest single vertical drop of all the Lakeland waterfalls. An interesting scramble can be made up the rocks to the base of the main fall, but it is not for the faint-hearted or for when the water is in spate and the rock slippery (especially with a tripod. . . believe me!).

Water-sculpted stones, veiled by the smooth passage of the stream, are one of the typical features of Lakeland becks.

Right. Dippers, unconcerned by the steady trickle of tourists, continually dart from the stream bed to nests high in the rock wall by Aira Force. In the early afternoon, especially after heavy rain, a rainbow forms and arches across the fall. Aira Force is reached by paths through a Victorian arboretum, managed by the National Trust. An old packhorse bridge spans the fall, and leaning over this to gaze at the tumultuous water crashing down the chasm is an unmissable experience.

The steep slopes of Walla Crag make this almost an aerial photograph of the ferry far below on Derwentwater. The autumn colours make a stark contrast with the dark lake.

The attractiveness of the set of waterfalls at the end of the Swindale valley amply repays the walk involved to reach them. These nine separate falls each have a distinctive character. In addition there are beautiful deep pools of soft dark peaty water, tempting spots in which to take a quick dip on hot days. Having lost some of its chill by running the length of Mosedale, the stream is relatively warm by Lakeland standards.

The fine view of the head of Ullswater
from Gowbarrow is one of my favourites.
Climbing Gowbarrow itself, despite it
having one of those not-yet-there
summits, is a good tonic for flagging
spirits and the view never ceases to
inspire me.

Right. Evening light floods across
Bassenthwaite Lake from the coastal
plain, illuminating Ullock Pike, Dodd
and the massive bulk of Skiddaw.
Bassenthwaite Lake now enjoys the
protection of being a National Nature
Reserve.

In the autumn, gossamer made up of fine cobwebs spun by small spiders can be found. This example, shimmering in early morning dew, was taken in Grizedale Forest.

In the series of sonnets From the River Duddon, Wordsworth describes its birth:
'. . . remote from every taint
Of sordid industry thy lot is cast'.
Two centuries later, the water of the Duddon still looks remarkably pure although airborne pollutants have no respect for National Park boundaries.

A slight ripple in the water made this reflection of reeds go quite jazzy. Angle Tarn, where this was taken, is a popular destination for walks from Patterdale. The quieter approach up over the hause from Boredale is a good way of seeing that undisturbed valley.

The long walk from Brotherilkeld up the Esk valley is an excellent approach to the Scafell range. However, the proximity of the river for most of the route is a great distraction, inviting many diversions to inspect the sparkling pools, the waterfalls and the packhorse bridge.

There is a high risk of never reaching Scafell. In fact on this occasion, I hardly even started.

Friar's Crag on Derwentwater is a
particularly popular viewpoint.

Pages 40, 41. This peaceful spring
morning on Esthwaite Water was soon
to be shattered by dozens of coarse
fishermen. Usually it is the fisherman
that is interrupted by the coarse
photographer.

Represented in countless paintings and photographs, the Buttermere Pines form a quintessential Lakeland scene. The rich colour of dead bracken adds a useful warmth to the photograph.

Scattered around the two main tarns on Haystacks, Innominate Tarn (shown here) and Blackbeck Tarn is a myriad of tiny tarns, some scarcely bigger than puddles. They all have individual qualities, and reflect those giants of the Lakeland fells, Great Gable, Kirkfell and Pillar.

Pages 44 and 45. Approaching storms inevitably have me dipping into my rucksack for waterproofs and heading hastily for a huddle under the nearest stone wall. These two storms, one above Bannerdale north of Blencathra, the other in the Lowther valley, had me reaching for my tripod instead. I was lucky that they passed me by.

CHRIS BONINGTON'S LAKE DISTRICT

Loughrigg Tarn, with its view to the Langdale Pikes, is one of my evening photographic haunts. Beware of the swan, which has a habit of muscling in on picnics and barbecues. It once gobbled a length of hot Cumberland sausage and we watched this, our supper, make its very visible way down the bird's neck.

Opposite. This tranquil dawn photograph belies the story behind the lake's name. Brotherswater is said to refer to the drowning of two brothers in the lake, although an alternative has Wordsworth parting from his brother here. Brotherswater was probably once part of Ullswater.

These obliging Herdwick sheep lined up to say 'cheese'. Ennerdale is very much a locals' lake. While on the foreshore, I met an amiable family who shared their tea with me. I asked if they had come far. 'Oh yes,' they replied, 'from Whitehaven!'

Ennerdale serves as a reservoir for West Cumbria, but remains relatively unspoilt by water extraction. However, this cow clearly hadn't read the nearby 'No Swimming' notice.

Within Grizedale Forest lie two large tarns. Both are on the routes of various walking and cycling trails made for visitors. Particularly worth seeing are the seventy or so sculptures commissioned by the Grizedale Society and created from materials found within the forest.

Below. The River Brathay flows sedately out of Elterwater at the start of its short journey to Windermere. It idles through wide pools past tree-topped hummocky hills, creating an idyllic scene. Shortly downstream, the pace of the river suddenly quickens and it plunges over Skelwith Force.

Right. I particularly welcome wonderful winter days. Not only is it good to spend a whole day outdoors but generally the light is better, and the colours more interesting than in the high summer. The water in this sheltered corner of Ullswater is frequently still.

Dead grasses, rimed by hoar frost, stand
out against the dark water of this pool
on the River Brathay. The low winter
sun never touched this particular spot
all day.

Photographing the sun rising over
Ullswater requires an early start on a
summer's morning. Watching the sun
rise and slowly light the landscape seems
far more satisfying than seeing it set. I
prefer not to use filters, but choose
instead to seek out conditions where the
colours are intense.

DAVID W. JONES   *A Privileged View*

David W. Jones is a freelance photographer specialising in traditional aspects of the Lake District. He says moving there from Manchester felt like winning the pools. He still feels that way. Like many photographers, he was initially attracted to the magnificent landscape but slowly he became fascinated with photographing the people of the area and the special skills and crafts which go to creating and preserving it. He has had several exhibitions of his work, especially his black and white photography.

Bill Hogarth, of Spark Bridge, makes these traditional 'Witch's broomstick' besoms from bundles of birch twigs with a stout hazel rod driven in to form the handle. This was once a traditional industry in the Lake District but now there are only a handful of people turning them out.

The Lakeland landscape offers a unique combination of the truly spectacular and the picturesque, enthralling visitors from many climes.

My photographs are an attempt to reveal the story which nestles within the scenic view. The life of the fell farmer, quarryman and waller, the coppice woodsman, swill basket maker and the remnants of once extensive rural industries such as bobbin making. Sports and shows, Cumberland and Westmorland wrestling and hound trails, traditional crafts and competitions all viewed critically, yet proudly, by the Cumbrian folk, who breed the distinctive Herdwick sheep.

I was drawn to record these traditional aspects of Lakeland in the late 1960s. At first I worked mainly in black and white. At this time there were still time-served craftsmen working, whose skills were acquired prior to the Second World War. They retained the dress and demeanour of their youth and I felt privileged to photograph them.

Perhaps the most significant of these photographic essays was of Stott Park Bobbin Mill. I was fortunate to photograph the mill in production. Little had altered since the 1920s with a workforce close to retirement. There was the opportunity to record scenes which gave combinations of original machinery, much of it manufactured in the area, sawdust coated windows and ankle deep wood shavings, peopled by men of character and charm.

Without the generous co-operation of the people performing their tasks I could not produce the pictures I desire. Special people such as George Birkett, a National Trust fell farmer who allowed me to photograph his year. Bill Hogarth, a coppice woodsman, master of many woodland skills. National Trust drystone wallers with whom I spent time earlier this summer and all the show officials and participants who offer their help and knowledge so willingly.

Working at VSEL at Barrow-in-Furness, I enter another world through my photography and it is one which fascinates and, I think, deserves to be recorded and treasured.

Ian Benson is a blacksmith working in Ambleside, right in the heart of one of the main tourist villages. When I visited him he was making gate supports for the National Trust to use in the drystone walls.

Tony Young re-lays his hedges at Moss End Farm, Lindale. The trunk of each bush is cut almost through so that it can be bent downwards and laid along the line of the hedge to create a tough, stockproof barrier. Because the trunks have been cut only part way through the hedge remains a living part of the countryside, providing food and shelter for wildlife.

Bill Hogarth has been a coppice woodsman in south Lakeland all his working life. For generations the trees were not felled but were cut and regenerated to ensure a constant supply of timber for various needs. Here Bill is peeling oak bark from a tree to be used in a traditional method of tanning leather. Once this would have been a common sight but now there are only a couple of traditional hand tanneries in the whole country.

Paul Girling is a chair bodger from Witherslack, in the Southern Lakes. 'Bodger' here should not be confused with the use elsewhere in the country where it can mean to make a terrible mess of things. In the woodlands a bodger is a very skilled man who makes furniture from the timber.

Paul Girling demonstrates his skill with the tools of a bodger. He is seated astride the mare and using a two-handed spoke shave to pare strips from this piece of wood which will become a leg for a chair.

Today quite a few people want to pick up the old woodland skills and Anne Frahm holds an annual weekend in the woods at Hay Bridge, Bouth, where people from all over the country come to learn from instructors like Bill Hogarth, Walter Lloyd and Owen Jones. This is a greenwood chair in the making.

Owen Jones, of Nibthwaite, is the last full-time swill maker, earning his living from this once widespread method of making traditional hard-wearing baskets. It is a time-consuming and cunning process which makes use of coppiced wood. Oak poles are bought from the bark peeler and then cut into quarters. After that the poles have to be boiled to make them more pliable and then are peeled into strips ready for weaving onto the wooden frame of the basket. It sounds a complicated process but once finished a well-made swill will last for years.

Walter Lloyd has spent many years living in the coppice woodlands of South Lakeland and practising a variety of woodland crafts. Here he is making wooden tent pegs which, though they have fallen out of favour with lightweight campers, are still in great demand by the army and for holding up the marquees at village shows and fetes.

CHRIS BONINGTON'S LAKE DISTRICT

The modern fashion for barbecues has given a considerable boost to charcoal making in the woods. Walter Lloyd was the first burner in the area to use the kiln method after the 1939–45 war. Here he empties one of his kilns as the other two smoulder away in the background.

Anyone who has read *Swallows and Amazons* will expect charcoal burners to be smoke-grimed men, so Sylvia Watthews, seen here in the Lyth Valley, will come as a bit of surprise. Sylvia was one of the first women charcoal burners in the country.

Drystone walls are an essential part of the Lakeland scenery, covering the fellsides like a web, following every fold of the ground. Building them without a speck of mortar is a skilled job that requires patience and a practised eye for picking up the right stone to slot into place. Each wall is really two walls which taper together at the top and are held together by 'throughs' which fit into both sides. The centre is packed with smaller stones and finally topped with cap stones. A good wall will last centuries but even the best needs attention to repair the ravages of weather and Herdwick sheep – not to mention walkers who try to climb over them. Ken Stephenson and Steve Jacques are National Trust wallers and have no shortage of work to keep them busy. Here they are working on a perfect day high in the Ennerdale Fells at Red Beck Close. The fells in the background are Bowness Knott and Herdus Scaw.

Left. Not all Lakeland's industries were picturesque and for centuries the Lake District was a mining and quarrying area, employing hundreds of people. The Coppermines above Coniston are a scheduled Historic Monument. This is the remains of the wheelpit of the old Red Dell Engine shaft. The Coppermines Valley is a popular route for walkers climbing the Old Man of Coniston.

Below. The Duddon Iron Furnace was one of several charcoal blast furnaces built in the early 18th century in south Lakeland. They used charcoal from the woods to smelt the iron ore which was mined locally while fast-running streams powered the water bellows.

Below. Slate quarrying has been a staple Lakeland industry for centuries. Neville Walker operates a circular saw at the High Fell Greenslate Company cutting blocks which have been quarried from National Trust-owned land at Tilberthwaite.

Right. Stott Park Bobbin Mill was one of the last of the traditional mills which turned out bobbins for the northern textile mills. It closed its doors in 1971 and is now an industrial museum operated by English Heritage. Stepping into the mill was like entering a time capsule, much of the machinery was from the last century and many of the workers of retirement age. Here foreman Jim Graham operates a small boring machine with a swill of bobbins in the foreground.

The quarries high up on the Old Man above Coniston are obvious signs of Lakeland's industrial past. The quarries have long since closed down but their legacy gives a distinctive atmosphere to the Old Man and his family of surrounding fells. The workings are a source of endless fascination – or aggravation, according to outlook – for walkers heading for the surrounding tops. Scattered across the valley and hillsides are remnants of the old industries. Here old rail and cableways, once used to transport the stone, still snake across the valley.

Once peat was the main fuel source for families in many parts of Lakeland. The peat would be cut from special workings and then left on the moor to dry before being taken back to the house. Here Edgar Park, from the Lyth Valley, and his son, Colin, are moving the peat on a special barrow.

Horse sales, like this one at George Denney's Johnscales Farm in the Lyth Valley, still attract plenty of interest. The horses are led around the ring so that the knowledgeable buyers and the merely curious can all get a good look at the animals before the serious bidding gets under way.

Right. Sheep farming is at the heart of life in the fells and lambing time is always busy for farmers like George Birkett of Birk How. George, with his ever-present crook and dog, carries a sickly lamb back to the farm where he can keep an eye on its progress.

Below. Winter is a hard time for both man and beast on Lakeland's hill farms, where winter can come early and linger long, but Kendal Rough Fells sheep are a hardy breed. They need to be, as snow covers the ground and storm clouds threaten another fall.

Lambing time on George Birkett's Birk How Farm means regular checks on the flock for new arrivals and to make sure ewes and lambs are thriving. Any that need special attention are brought closer to the farm where progress can be watched more carefully. Birk How is one of many farms in Lakeland owned by the National Trust which are run using traditional methods.

Hound trailing is one of the most keenly-contested Lakeland sports. Most valley shows include at least one trail and many farmers keep a hound or two. The race begins with the 'slip' when the hounds are released by their owners to follow a trail which has been laid across the fells using an aniseed-soaked rag.

The trailer makes the course as difficult as possible crossing fences, drystone walls and even small crags on his way. Trails for novice hounds can be quite short but full-grown hounds may race up to ten miles before they get back to the start where owners shout, whistle and wave tins of 'bait' to spur the hungry

dogs to a final effort. The keenness of the competition among owners is matched only by the liveliness of the betting around the showground as owners and spectators wait for the first sight of the hounds coming into view over a ridge and rushing down the fellside to the finish.

Below. Fell racing is one of the most gruelling sports and is often a race of two halves as the runners toil up the steepest slopes to the top of the nearest fell and round a marker flag before dashing headlong down the slopes at astonishing speed. All the runners have to be fit but many a good climber has seen his apparently commanding lead at the top of the hill overtaken by a specialist at high speed descents. This runner at Eskdale Show has the spectacular Scafell range and Bow Fell behind him.

CHRIS BONINGTON'S LAKE DISTRICT

Left. The Shepherd's Crook competition always attracts plenty of attention at Lakeland shows and Wasdale Show is no exception. Farmers' everyday crooks are working tools and do not have this elaborate decoration but these highly carved crooks are prized possessions and competition is fierce. Great Gable forms a magnificent backcloth to the judging.

Cumberland and Westmorland Wrestling is the most famous of the local sports. This most skilful of contests is said to trace its roots back to the Vikings. Two men face each other and 'tak hod' by locking their arms behind each other's backs. The aim is to topple the opponent to the ground. If both fall the one on the bottom loses. To the uninitiated not much may seem to be happening as the wrestlers struggle for the advantage but cunning often beats strength at this surprisingly subtle sport. The costume is traditional, featuring vest and long johns with decorated trunks. Most contests feature prizes for the best dressed wrestler.

The Furness Morris Men perform at many of the shows in south Lakeland as well as performing traditional Pace Egg plays at Easter. Morris men often perform at pubs and have a reputation for proving it to be thirsty work. Young William Spain prefers an ice cream as he takes a break at Lowick Show.

Opposite. Bill Airey, of Lakeside at the southern end of Windermere, is a coppice wood burner and charcoal burner.

JULIE FRYER   *A Cluster of Jewels*

Julie Fryer was given her first camera at the age of ten and has enjoyed taking photographs ever since. But it was not until she moved to Wigton in Cumbria in 1980 that she was able to satisfy her ambition to become a landscape photographer. Since then she has walked hundreds of miles over the Lakeland fells and valleys – and hung around for hundreds of hours waiting for the right light – capturing the district in all its moods.

The complete stillness of this summit tarn on Haystacks on a February day appealed to me. It is a tarn which can look very different from different directions but with the mist just creeping up and the rocks reflected in the water it looks very tranquil.

If you travel the whole length of the Lake District along the main roads, from Bothel in the North to Newby Bridge in the South, and then check the length of your journey, you will find it to be about forty-five miles. Yet within that distance there is a huge contrast and variation in the landscape. From open countryside swept by the winds off the Solway Firth, suddenly and spectacularly you are among mountains, passing under two of England's highest peaks and alongside five lakes (or to be accurate, one lake, one water and three meres). The skyline changes constantly; there are pointed peaks, rounded, wooded hills, coniferous forests, outcrops of bare rock, lush valley pastures, streams tumbling down the fell sides, farmhouses, dry stone walls, plus three small towns which have managed so far (I think) to avoid impinging too stridently upon the land around them. And then the high country ceases as quickly as it began, and you are again in a softer, pastoral environment.

This very compactness is what to me makes the Lake District special; within a remarkably confined area there is an abundance of wonderfully varied scenic riches, a small but precious cluster of jewels set in the map of England.

And, like jewels, the Lake District needs light for its beauties to be fully appreciated. Any frequent visitor to this area will know that the views seen on the journey described above could well be all but obliterated in the rain, low cloud and hill fog which form a regular part of the Cumbrian weather.

But when the clouds clear and the sun does come out, then for me the landscape is really revealed. All its features – the volcanic upheavals and glacial action which resulted in the rock forms and the mountain and valley contours that we know today, and the centuries of man's manipulation of that terrain – all this is illuminated by the light. Rocky peaks stand out vividly against a blue sky, and lengthening shadows throw stone walls, buildings, trees, and the shapes and folds of the hillsides into sharp relief, and also make their own graphic patterns on the land. Calm, hazy conditions contrast with the biting visual clarity produced by a north-west wind, and each reveals a different facet of the physical environment.

In this selection of photographs I have concentrated on the high ground of the Lake District. As a walker, rather than a climber, I love being among the rocks and crags of the high fells. Surely for a walker, the chief joy in the Lake District is to be able to experience, within the span of a couple of hours, such a contrasting but always beautiful range of scenery, from the fertile softness of the valleys, through the intermediate rising ground where the vegetation becomes sparser and the trees cling

ever more precariously to the sheltered gill sides, to the rough and airy tops and ridges, from where the valleys and lakes are again visible, strung out gem-like far below, their place in the physical scheme of things made clear.

This is a landscape to be preserved at all costs.

Left. This very striking cairn is not on the actual summit of Lingmell. It is just a bit to the west of it but it is magnificently built. It was a very hot and hazy afternoon and I love the way the fells behind seem to be layered in paler bands of colour.

Below. I think it is a great pity we don't still have the old counties of Cumberland, Westmorland and Lancashire-North-of-the-Sands. This stone post, known as the Three Shire Stone, near the summit of Wrynose Pass, is the only place where the three old counties touched.

The Langdale Pikes seem to be visible from most summits in Lakeland. This view of them from Blea Tarn is not taken from the traditional viewpoint. Instead I squelched out into the marshy ground by the water's edge. I particularly like the contrast between the wildflowers in the foreground and the jagged peaks behind. I wanted to get the reflections in the tarn but the area is quite high so the water here is very rarely still. I went four times before I found the conditions I wanted early one June morning. Even so I got there with only a few minutes to spare. Just after I took the photograph a breeze got up and the reflections vanished in the ripples.

For unfit people like me the walk up Grains Gill from Seathwaite to Esk Hause is very much relieved by glorious views back to Borrowdale and the meanderings of the gill along the way. This waterfall halfway up is one of my favourite places. I love the overhanging tree and the colour of the water.

When I've been on the tops around Grasmoor, Gasgale Gill makes a very soothing descent, following the stream down from Coledale Hause. This picture was taken on a September evening when the rocks and water were catching the low, warm light.

CHRIS BONINGTON'S LAKE DISTRICT

This was a chilly day in March with a fierce-looking sky over Bow Fell and the Crinkles, but the sunshine down in the valley was very bright picking up the green of the fields and the stones at the edge of the River Esk. Eskdale is a Jekyll and Hyde valley. It is pastoral in its lower reaches but the head of the valley is one of the wildest places in the Lakes.

From this traditional Cumberland house near Caldbeck the land just drops away to the Solway Plain. It looks as if it is sitting on the edge of the world. In the background you can see straight across to Scotland beyond the Solway Firth. Any house there must be very robustly built to withstand the constant westerlies that sweep in off the Irish Sea.

Bulatt Bridge by Burnmoor Tarn is on the old corpse road along which families in Wasdale used to carry their dead to consecrated ground in Eskdale before Wasdale had its own burial ground.

There are all sorts of spooky legends about vanishing corpses, and standing on this bridge it is easy to believe they are all true.

There is not much for the sheep on top of Scafell Pike, seen here from Ill Crag on the route from Esk Hause. There is very little grass and an unremitting grey sea of rock and boulders along the whole ridge, which, as Wainwright says, makes for very hard going.

Left. I think this is one of the most inviting scenes in the Lake District with a public footpath starting from the road at Stoneycroft in the Newlands Valley and the delectable-looking summit of Causey Pike in view.

Below. Scales Tarn sits in an upland basin below Blencathra. The path on the left goes up to the rocky ridge of Sharp Edge. On a sunny day like this it has a benign appearance but on a grey day it is a gloomy spot.

Although the Langdale Pikes are relatively low, they always look impressive mountains because of the steep face they present to Langdale. Pike of Stickle, the most westerly of the group, has one of the most distinctive and sharpest summits in Lakeland, rising in a sugarloaf from the plateau before plunging almost 2,000 feet down the screes into the green valley of Mickleden below. Fortunately, despite its forbidding appearance, there is an easy scramble to the summit for walkers.

Right. Blencathra rises like a primeval beast from the A66 with huge ridges running down to the green fields of the Vale of Keswick. The most exciting of the ridges is the central one, Hall's Fell, which leads directly to the summit. The ridge is twisting, steep and narrow. Often the path avoids the craggiest pinnacles but if you want a bit of fun you can climb right along the crest. The contrast between the wild terrain of the mountain and green of the valley, which is always in view, becomes ever more pronounced the higher you climb.

Below. There are several Eagle Crags in Lakeland but this one above Stonethwaite in Borrowdale is easily the most striking. Walkers who take the track in the foreground have a choice of going left to Greenup Edge or right into Langstrath. I like the way the bare branches of the tree stand out starkly against the shadow of the fell.

Left. Bowfell Buttress is a very imposing piece of rock close to the summit of the mountain. It has one of the classic rock climbs in the Lake District which one party considered so perfect that instead of continuing their walk they climbed up and down it all day. I'm happy just to stand and look at it.

Wasdale Head is a tremendous place. You can stand on the green and be surrounded by massive fells from Yewbarrow and Pillar, to Kirk Fell, Great Gable, Lingmell and the Scafells but tucked away behind the hotel is this glorious little packhorse bridge. This view is looking up the beck with Kirk Fell rising behind.

Seatoller, at the foot of the Honister Pass, seems to epitomise the idea of a village nestling in the fells. This was taken early in November, which is often the best time for colours, and here the light is just catching the trees by the roadside and contrasting them with the bright white of the buildings and the weathered stone walls.

Left. A lot of drivers must have been mighty relieved to get here. This is the top of Hardknott, the most notorious pass in Lakeland with hairpin bends and 1-in-3 gradients. If you are on your way to Ambleside the fun and games haven't finished because you still have to negotiate Wrynose Pass, which can be seen in the background.

Below. There are many days in the Lake District when you can walk on the fells and not see anything because of the low cloud. I thought this was going to be one of those days but when I got to the top of Red Pike the cloud suddenly lifted and a shaft of sunlight lit up Buttermere village far below.

This shot was taken in the pouring rain, looking down the Watendlath Valley from the hamlet, but I think the light is quite magical. This hanging valley above Borrowdale has been inhabited since prehistoric times and it is fascinating to think that early settlers must have found their way up this valley to the tarn above.

This is the farm at Wasdale Head with the bulk of Lingmell towering behind. I like the contrast between the typically rural valley scene in the foreground and the rugged slopes behind. This is something you come across again and again in the Lake District with the valley farms hemmed in by high fells.

Pages 104, 105. I took this picture not so much for the view of Eagle Crag as for the shapes. I loved the curving sheepfold and the way it echoed the slopes of the surrounding fells.

This is an unusual view of the Langdale Pikes from the ridge between Glaramara and Allen Crags. It shows that despite the formidable front they present to Langdale the hinterland of these striking peaks is a high upland plateau. The Coniston Fells beyond Little Langdale present a far more shapely outline.

This is one of my favourite views in Lakeland, which I have photographed many times. The church in the foreground, St Bartholomew's, is in Loweswater Parish but the lake behind is Crummock Water while Grasmoor forms an imposing and rugged backdrop.

Even in the middle of nowhere you still have to do the chores. I was struck by the contrast of this wild setting and the domesticity of the washing hung out between the trees.

Both these views show the softening effects of haze in the Lakeland landscape. While the trees and shrubs in the foregrounds stand out sharply, the fells behind fade to pastel shades lending a dreamlike quality. The shapely top of Grizedale Pike rises beyond Bassenthwaite Lake behind the solitary tree on Dodd summit, while in the other picture the shape of Fairfield echoes the lines of Silver Crag under Place Fell.

Calm winter days can produce views of startling clarity. Two of the most striking fells in the Lake District, Fleetwith Pike (right) and Skiddaw (below), are seen at their best here reflected in the still waters of Buttermere and Derwentwater. These pictures were both taken in the early afternoon and within an hour the light had faded and darkness began to fall.

Right. During summer the summit of Helvellyn is a busy place with a constant procession of visitors, a good number of whom sit on the stone seats in the windshelter to have their lunch. In winter when the winds blow across the plateau and fill the shelter with snowdrifts it takes on an Arctic appearance.

Below. Seen from Whiteside after a heavy snowfall, Gasgale Gill snakes down into the valley from Coledale Hause with the ridge to Hopegill Head on the left skyline and the slopes of Grasmoor plunging down steeply on the right.

Left. This was not the clearest of days but I liked the ethereal quality of the light in this view of the Coniston Fells taken at dusk from Loughrigg with the sun just catching Elterwater in the valley below.

Below. In winter the whole of the Helvellyn range takes on an almost Alpine appearance with snow clinging to the shadowed north east faces. The snow can form impressive cornices and lingers long in coves which are sheltered from the westerly winds and hold snow long after the covering on the higher Scafells has melted. Under these conditions the coves of Dollywagon Pike are a playground for mountaineers but a dangerous temptation to the unwary.

My abiding memory of standing here at the summit of Wrynose Pass to take this picture looking towards Hardknott was that the smell of burning rubber hung heavy in the air. Those who found the serpentine twists of Hardknott in the background too daunting could always turn left at Cockley Beck to sneak off down the gentle Duddon Valley.

On the day this photograph was taken
the weatherman had promised clear blue
skies and no cloud. For once I was
pleased that he was wrong otherwise
I would have missed standing on Green
Gable with this lovely view of Pillar and
Pillar Rock with swathes of cloud and
mist playing over the ridges.

BRIAN HIBBERT   *Glorious Harmony*

Brian Hibbert came to photography through his love of fell walking. A year after he began walking he bought his first camera to try to capture the views he saw. Since then his photographic equipment has expanded until now it is usual for him to carry at least 20lbs of cameras, lenses and the tripod which he always uses when he takes to the hills. His work has featured in most of the major outdoor magazines as well as on calendars and in photographic journals.

One of the many pleasures of taking the old valley paths in the Lake District is that so many of them cross beautifully-made old packhorse bridges. This one is at Bridge End, Smaithwaite, near Thirlmere. The steep rock face behind is Raven Crag.

Lakeland is, in parts, a wilderness. High among the mountains and on the wild upland moors, evidence of Man is hard to find. But there are signs of Man's brief intrusion in the building of summit cairns, in the packhorse trails, in the miners' and quarrymen's paths, in the old drove roads that lead from the mountains to the valleys below and in the standing stones and stone circles which date from pre-historic times. Apart from these relics, the landscape remains the same today as it appeared millions of years ago.

Below the intake walls, the interaction between Man and nature is revealed in its fullest glory. There are farms built from roughly hewn stone, the texture of which is sharply picked out in raking Lakeland light. There are picturesque packhorse bridges that span lively becks. There are isolated shepherds' cottages dwarfed by towering rocky heights. There are field barns and drystone wall enclosures that contrast strongly with the more sombre background of shadowy crags. White-washed chapels sheltered in secluded glades and brilliant red rural post-boxes add dramatic impact to otherwise flat scenes. And though there is little sense of conformity here – the dwellings in the hamlets and villages are charmingly haphazard – all is in harmony.

Man fashioned the Lakeland landscape from the moment he first settled within it back in the eighth and ninth centuries and he has not done a bad job. For this, we should thank the landowners, tenant farmers past and present and the National Trust. Man has not, however, been entirely blameless. The ugly scars and the naked ruins of abandoned mines and quarries are prime examples of his presence, though most sites are now returning to nature. The overwhelming problems threatening Lakeland's future are now posed by tourism and the motor car. I hope we do not destroy that which took so long to create.

St John's in the Vale is one of those little valleys that not too many people use so the road and the paths are still relatively quiet. This lovely old ivy-clad bridge crosses St John's Beck and the peaceful scene under the trees contrasts with the steep slopes of Bram Crag behind.

Wasdale Head is one of those places where at first glance everything seems to be on show. As you drive into the valley you see the Screes and the trio of Yewbarrow, Gable and Lingmell grouped around the head of the lake. This little bridge is tucked away behind the hotel but it is well worth seeking out.

Thousands upon thousands of walkers use High Sweden Bridge to cross Scandale Beck every year. It is the start – or finish depending which way round you go – of the classic Fairfield Horseshoe, a tough walk of a dozen or so miles.

This odd-looking building at Shoulthwaite near Thirlmere is a shooting hide which is used for culling deer. It's a strange sight to come across in the Lake District but it stands out nicely against Iron Crag in this picture.

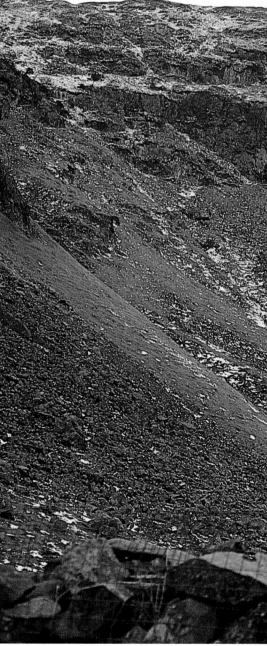

CHRIS BONINGTON'S LAKE DISTRICT

Left. Traditional whitewashed buildings pick up the sunshine and put life into a picture. This group is at Little Langdale.

Below. Tarn Hows near Coniston is a bit of a strange place because it is a man-made beauty spot in the middle of a huge area of natural beauty. A lot of visitors don't realise it was created by damming marshy ground to create the tarn.

Right. If ever there was a 'Christmas card' shot this is it. What else could you post in this box in Great Langdale?

Below. This boat tied up under the trees at Watergate at the southern end of Loweswater looks as though it is just waiting for someone to come along for a spot of fishing.

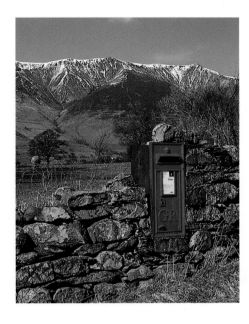

Left. This post box beneath Blencathra looks as though it has seen a fair bit of use and the wall around it is showing signs of wear. It makes a contrast with the solid permanence of the huge wall of ridges and gullies on the mountain behind it. I like to get a bit of red into landscapes so a post box is always useful for that.

Below. Stott Park Bobbin Mill is an amazing place which is now run as a museum. It is still run as it was when it closed in 1971 but when you go in it is almost impossible to believe that people were working there in the 1970s. To a modern visitor it seems Dickensian.

Not all the bridges in the Lake District are old. Some of the new paths need modern bridges but this wooden footbridge at Nichol Dub, near Seatoller in Borrowdale, has been made to blend in with the wooded surroundings of the valley. Nature's helping things along with the lichen which is colonising the woodwork.

Left. When people come to the Lake District they expect to find nothing but drystone walls. Down in the valleys there are plenty of hedges and quite a few of railings, nicely set off in this picture by the low sunlight through the tree.

Burnmoor Tarn, on the old corpse road from Wasdale to Eskdale, was described by Wainwright as a large and unattractive sheet of water in a desolate landscape. On a sunny day like this it does not look too bad but it was a lonely existence for the keeper at Burnmoor Lodge beside the tarn.

Most Lakeland farms have no shortage of stone and most buildings were made of what was immediately to hand. The result is that they seem to have just grown out of the land itself. This barn at Hartsop in Patterdale seems to have settled itself down comfortably in a fold of the ground under the tree and pulled a blanket of moss and heather over itself.

CHRIS BONINGTON'S LAKE DISTRICT

This path to Combe Gill on Glaramara
leaves the main road through
Borrowdale close to Mountain View
Cottages. The little bridge hiding in
the trees is reached quite soon but the
thing that attracted me to this picture
was the solitary foxglove catching the
light by the boulder.

Michael's Fold, like so much near
Grasmere, claims a connection with
Wordsworth. In his poem about
Michael the shepherd Wordsworth
described the nearby Greenhead Ghyll,
but after heavy rain this 'tumultuous
brook' might fit the part just as well.
The tiny bridge seems almost too fragile
to walk on.

Of all Man's works in Lakeland, Castlerigg Stone Circle is one of the most mysterious. Although nowhere near as tall as Stonehenge, the circle is virtually complete with thirty-one perimeter stones and another eight forming a rectangle inside. Although it is more than 4,000 years old arguments still go on over what it was used for. Most people now believe it was used as an astronomical clock, following the movements of the sun and stars to plot the agricultural year. Whatever its origins it remains a place with a special atmosphere.

Middle Fell Farm sits at the end of
Great Langdale where the road finally
gives up the ghost and slinks away over
Blea Tarn, leaving the valley to walkers
heading for Bow Fell and Crinkle Crags.
It is a traditional whitewashed farm with
a sturdy porch that could turn the biting
winds that can funnel down the valley
even on a sunny afternoon like this.

Some parts of the country have a distinctive style of church that marks them out. Not the Lake District. The valleys are all subtly different and are populated by people who have their own ideas about how things should be done. Their churches reflect those differences. But all have one thing in common. Like the people who built them they are sturdy, not much given to fancy show and are capable of standing up to the worst weather the mountains can throw

at them. Towers, where they exist at all, are squat and solid, with none of the self-important spires to be found in the plump parishes of the softer lowlands. Naves are kept big enough to fit their congregations but not so grand as to harbour unnecessary cold and draughts. The four churches here are at Kirkstile, top left; Cartmell Fell, bottom left; Troutbeck, top right and Dacre, bottom right.

Borrowdale is one of the most popular valleys for visitors but even here it is possible to find deserted pathways and tracks. This one is near Rosthwaite where the valley opens out again after passing through the Jaws.

Left. This is not quite the usual view of the Langdale Pikes. It was taken from the opposite side of the valley from the road and gives a view into Stickle Gill. A pitched path has now been laid beside the stream, leading from Stickle Tarn.

Below. Hardknott Fort above Eskdale guarded the Romans' trading route from their fort at Ambleside to the port of Ravenglass. It occupies a commanding position over the valley but must have seemed a grim posting for soldiers brought to Britain from the warmer parts of the empire.

This walled track leads from Wood Close, near Grasmere, to Grey Crag but the way the walls twist and turn suggests they are in no hurry to get there. Even the track worn in grass follows its own zig-zag route instead of going in a simple straight line.

The men who made the old trackways knew a thing or two about walking uphill. Some of today's walkers create paths which attack slopes head on – though they usually make them on the way downhill rather than by going uphill. The men who climbed the hills

for business rather than pleasure knew how to work with the land to minimise their effort and save their strength. This cleverly constructed track above the hidden valley of St John's in the Vale makes use of a shelf above the crag to make the climb easier. The wall emphasises the line of the track with the bare tree standing like a sentinel on the corner.

Right. Smaithwaite is a surprisingly quiet spot near the northern end of Thirlmere. The barn is just catching the light and is echoed by the sunshine on the fells in the background.

Below. These days farmers seem to prefer making silage, getting the grass cut and baled as quickly as possible, so it is a bit of a treat to see a hayfield drying in the sun like this one at Boredale to the east of Ullswater.

Left. Somebody must have built these walls near Rosthwaite in Borrowdale but with the moss growing over them they seem to be half-plants themselves. This track is actually part of the Cumbria Way footpath that runs for seventy miles from Ulverston to Carlisle.

Below. Not all Man's intrusions are as picturesque as the packhorse bridges. The woods and fells around Tilberthwaite are riddled with caves and quarries, a legacy of the old slate industry. But nature is slowly reclaiming many of them.

At certain times, but especially in the
early morning, the valleys can fill with
mist so the tops seem to be floating on a
insubstantial sea of clouds. This view
over Rydal is taken from the hills above
Ambleside.

Haweswater is one of the lakes that was created as a reservoir to slake Manchester's thirst. When the valley was dammed the village of Mardale was drowned but during droughts, like the ones in the mid-nineties, the water level drops and people flock to see what is left of the old village.

Of all the bridges in the Lake District, Ashness Bridge on the road to Watendlath must be the most painted and photographed and it is hardly surprising. No matter how hard you try to resist it, on a perfect late autumn day with the sun on the stonework, the bracken a warm gold, and Skiddaw with a dusting of snow behind, you just have to take the picture.

Left. Gatesgarth Pass, which linked the old village of Mardale, now drowned in Haweswater Reservoir with Longsleddale, is quiet at the best of times but especially on a day like this. Upper Longsleddale was the province of quarrymen in the old days.

Below. There are several popular low level walks around Tilberthwaite and Little Langdale and most of them make a point of crossing the delightful little Slater Bridge near the outflow of Little Langdale Tarn. It is so narrow that someone has wisely added a railing.